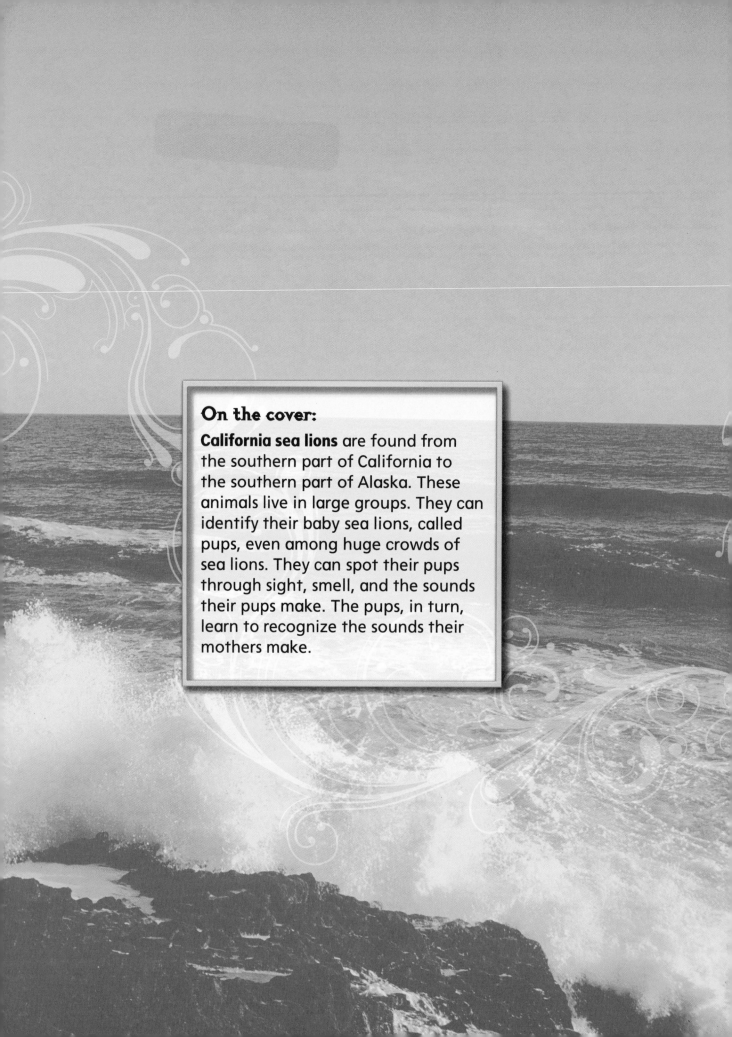

On the cover:

California sea lions are found from the southern part of California to the southern part of Alaska. These animals live in large groups. They can identify their baby sea lions, called pups, even among huge crowds of sea lions. They can spot their pups through sight, smell, and the sounds their pups make. The pups, in turn, learn to recognize the sounds their mothers make.

California Treasures

A Reading/Language Arts Program

Program Authors

Diane August
Donald R. Bear
Janice A. Dole
Jana Echevarria
Douglas Fisher
David Francis
Vicki Gibson
Jan E. Hasbrouck
Scott G. Paris
Timothy Shanahan
Josefina V. Tinajero

Macmillan/McGraw-Hill

Contributors

Time Magazine, Accelerated Reader

learning through listening

Students with print disabilities may be eligible to obtain an accessible, audio version of the pupil edition of this textbook. Please call Recording for the Blind & Dyslexic at 1-800-221-4792 for complete information.

A

The McGraw·Hill Companies

 Macmillan/McGraw-Hill

Published by Macmillan/McGraw-Hill, of McGraw-Hill Education, a division of The McGraw-Hill Companies, Inc., Two Penn Plaza, New York, New York 10121.

Printed in the United States of America

ISBN: 978-0-02-199965-1/1, Bk. 5
MHID: 0-02-199965-1/1, Bk. 5
1 2 3 4 5 6 7 8 9 (027/055) 12 11 10 09 08

Welcome to
California *Treasures*

Imagine having a pet dinosaur who wants to go to school, learning about how *real* animals act as teams, or reading about a kitten who thinks the moon is a bowl of milk. Your **Student Book** contains these and other award-winning fiction and nonfiction selections.

Treasures Meets California Standards

The instruction provided with each reading selection in your **Student Book** will ensure that you meet all the **California Reading/Language Arts Standards** for your grade. Throughout the book, special symbols (such as) and codes (such as **R 1.1.2**) have been added to show where and how these standards are being met. They will help you know *what* you are learning and *why*.

What do these symbols mean?

CA = Tested Standards in California

 = Skill or Strategy that will appear on your test

R = Reading Standards

W = Writing Standards

LC = Language Conventions Standards

LAS = Listening and Speaking Standards

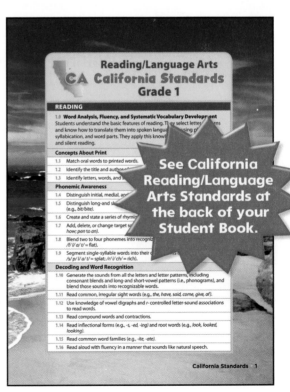

Reading/Language Arts
CA California Standards
Grade 1

READING

1.0 Word Analysis, Fluency, and Systematic Vocabulary Development
Students understand the basic features of reading. They select letter patterns and know how to translate them into spoken language by using phonics, syllabication, and word parts. They apply this knowledge to achieve fluent oral and silent reading.

Concepts About Print
1.1 Match oral words to printed words.
1.2 Identify the title and author of a reading selection.
1.3 Identify letters, words, and sentences.

Phonemic Awareness
1.4 Distinguish initial, medial, and final sounds in single-syllable words.
1.5 Distinguish long-and short-vowel sounds in orally stated single-syllable words (e.g., *bit/bite*).
1.6 Create and state a series of rhyming words, including consonant blends.
1.7 Add, delete, or change target sounds to change words (e.g., change *cow* to *how; pan to an*).
1.8 Blend two to four phonemes into recognizable words (e.g., /c/ a/ t/ = cat; /f/ l/ a/ t/ = flat).
1.9 Segment single-syllable words into their components (e.g., /c/ a/ t/ = cat; /s/ p/ l/ a/ t/ = splat; /r/ i/ ch/ = rich).

Decoding and Word Recognition
1.10 Generate the sounds from all the letters and letter patterns, including consonant blends and long-and short-vowel patterns (i.e., phonograms), and blend those sounds into recognizable words.
1.11 Read common, irregular sight words (e.g., *the, have, said, come, give, of*).
1.12 Use knowledge of vowel digraphs and r-controlled letter-sound associations to read words.
1.13 Read compound words and contractions.
1.14 Read inflectional forms (e.g., -s, -ed, -ing) and root words (e.g., *look, looked, looking*).
1.15 Read common word families (e.g., -ite, -ate).
1.16 Read aloud with fluency in a manner that sounds like natural speech.

California Standards 1

See California Reading/Language Arts Standards at the back of your Student Book.

Mc Graw Hill **Macmillan/McGraw-Hill**

Unit 5

Science
Nature Watch

The Big Question

What can we learn about the world of nature?

Theme
Launcher
Video

 Find out more about nature at
www.macmillanmh.com.

The
Big
Question

What can we learn about the world of nature?

READ TOGETHER

The world of nature is all around us. It is up in the sky, in the trees, and under the ground. Plants, animals, the sky, water, and sunshine are all part of nature.

There are lots of things to study in nature. You can study the night sky. You can learn about the weather and what makes a day sunny or rainy. You can study animals and why they do the things they do. Learning about nature can help us understand the world around us. It also shows us how to take better care of the world. It can even show us some things about ourselves.

Research Activities

Is there a plant or animal you would like to learn about? Choose a plant or animal you find interesting. Find out as much as you can about it. Write down what you have learned. Share your report with the class.

Keep Track of Ideas

As you read, keep track of what you are learning about the world of nature on the Accordion organizer. You may want to include the weather, seasons, animals, plants, earth, and sky. Write what you are learning about each.

FOLDABLES®
Study Organizer

Weather Seasons Animals Plants The Sky The Earth

Research Toolkit

Conduct Your Unit 5 Research Online with:

Research Roadmap
Follow step-by-step guide to complete your research project.

Online Resources
- Topic Finder and other Research Tools
- Videos and Virtual Fieldtrips
- Photos and Drawings for Presentations
- Related Articles and Web Resources

California Web Site Links

Go to **www.macmillanmh.com** for more information.

California People

Dr. Sally Ride, Astronaut and Scientist
Sally Ride was the first woman astronaut in the United States. Today she is a scientist and teacher.

In the Sky

CA **Talk About It**

What can you see when you look up at the sky?

LOG ON ▶ Find out more about the sky at www.macmillanmh.com.

⭐ **Words to Know**

poor

through

climbed

another

full

---

leaped

lucky

Read to Find Out

What happens when Lily Rat goes out at night?

Lucky Lily

"Rats should not go out," all the rats said. "We saw a big cat."

But Lily Rat was so hungry. "**Poor** me!" she said.

She peeked **through** her hole. She saw a hunk of cheese on the shelf. It looked so good!

She ran out and **climbed** up the shelf. She had one bite of cheese. Then she had **another**. As she ate, she looked out at the night sky. It was so pretty!

Soon she was **full**. She **leaped** off the shelf and ran home.

What a night!

"I am a **lucky** rat," Lily said.

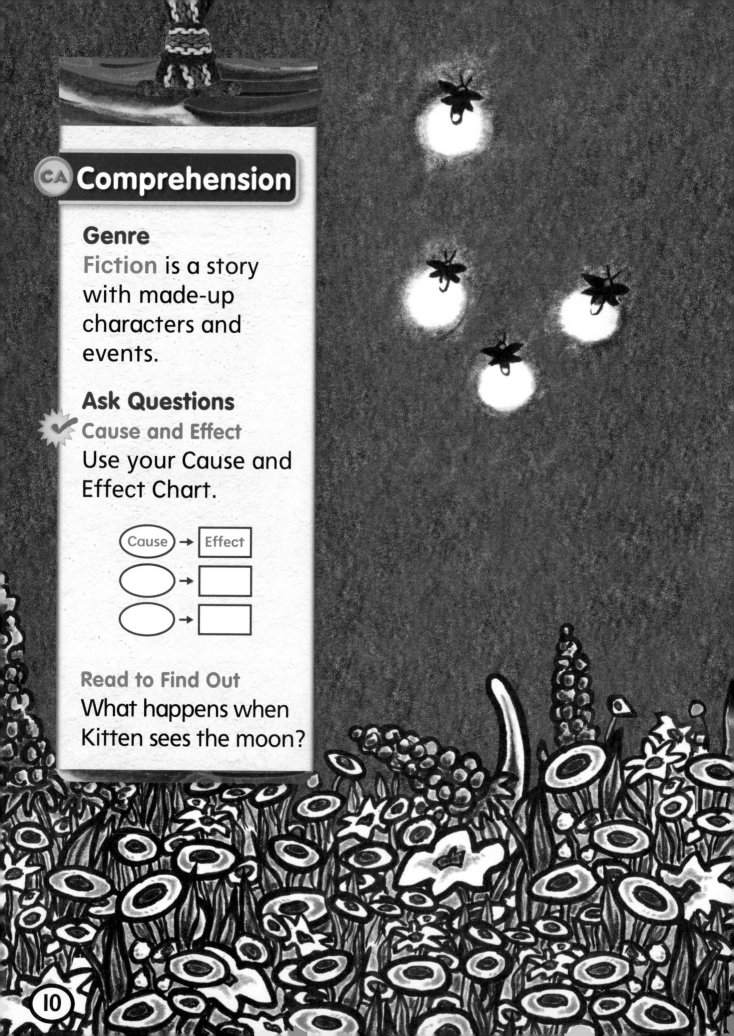

CA Comprehension

Genre
Fiction is a story with made-up characters and events.

Ask Questions
Cause and Effect
Use your Cause and Effect Chart.

Cause → Effect

Read to Find Out
What happens when Kitten sees the moon?

Kitten's First Full Moon

written and illustrated by
KEVIN HENKES

Award
Winning
Author/
Illustrator

It was Kitten's first full moon.

When she saw it, she thought,

There's a little bowl of milk in the sky.

And she wanted it.

So she closed her eyes

and stretched her neck

and opened her mouth and licked.

But Kitten only ended up
with a bug on her tongue.
Poor Kitten!

Still, there was the little bowl

of milk, just waiting.

So she pulled herself together

and wiggled her bottom

and sprang from the top step of the porch.

But Kitten only tumbled—

bumping her nose and banging her ear

and pinching her tail.

Poor Kitten!

Still, there was the little bowl

of milk, just waiting.

So she chased it—

down the sidewalk,

through the garden,

past the field,

and by the pond.

But Kitten never seemed to get

closer.

Poor Kitten!

Still, there was the little bowl

of milk, just waiting.

So she ran
to the tallest tree
she could find,
and she **climbed**
and climbed
and climbed
to the very top.

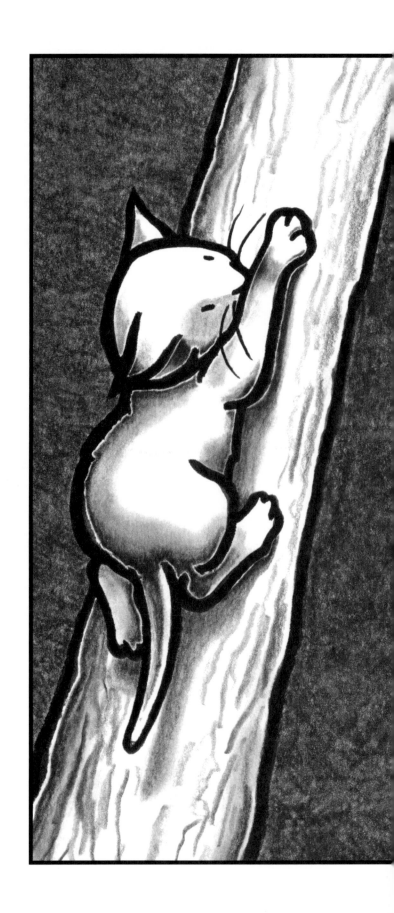

But Kitten
still couldn't reach
the bowl of milk,
and now she was
scared.
Poor Kitten!
What could she do?

Then, in the pond, Kitten saw
another bowl of milk.
And it was bigger.
What a night!

So she raced down the tree and

raced through the grass

and raced to the edge of the pond.

She leaped with all her might—

Poor Kitten!

She was wet and sad and tired
and hungry.

So she went

back home—

and there was

a great big

bowl of milk

   on the porch,

just waiting for her.

Lucky Kitten!

Kevin and Kitten

Kevin Henkes got the idea for *Kitten's First Full Moon* from a story he had begun to write many years before. Although he never finished this story, there was a line that read, "The cat thought the moon was a bowl of milk." He couldn't get this line out of his head, and slowly over the years the story of *Kitten's First Full Moon* formed.

Other books by Kevin Henkes

LOG ON ▶ Find out more about Kevin Henkes at **www.macmillanmh.com**.

Owen
KEVIN HENKES

Lilly's Big Day
KEVIN HENKES

CA **Author's Purpose**

Kevin Henkes got his story idea from a line he liked. Can you think of a line from a rhyme or story that you like? Draw and write about it.

Critical Thinking

Retell the Story

Use the Retelling Cards
to retell the story in order.

Retelling Cards

Think and Compare

1. What causes Kitten to chase the moon? What causes Kitten to jump into the pond?

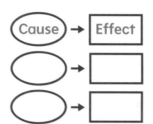

2. Have you ever tried to get something that was hard to reach as Kitten does? What happened?

3. Does the moon always look like a bowl of milk? How does the moon change?

4. How is Kitten like Lily in "Lucky Lily"?

Ellen Ochoa IN SPACE

Ellen Ochoa is an **astronaut.** She has been on many trips into space.

4

Ellen thinks space trips are exciting. She likes to see Earth from space. She sees our **planet** as the spacecraft climbs through the sky. And she sees the moon and stars at night. What a beautiful sight that is!

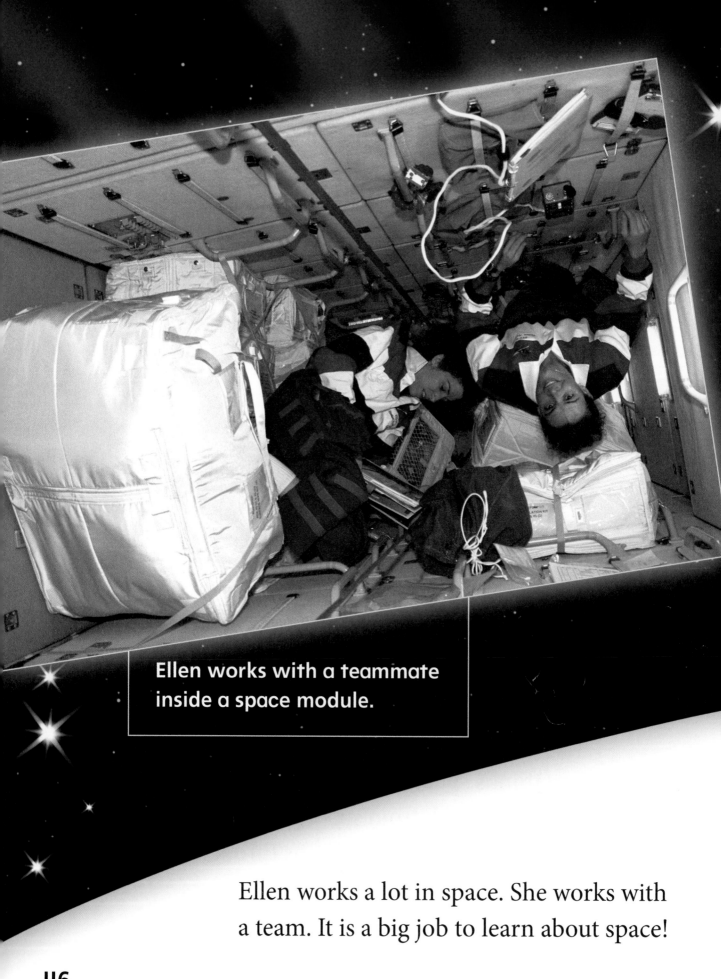

Ellen works with a teammate inside a space module.

Ellen works a lot in space. She works with a team. It is a big job to learn about space!

This is space food.
Ellen adds hot or cold
water to the pack.

In space, everything is **weightless**.
Everything floats!

So how can astronauts eat? Ellen has a tray
that sticks to her lap. Dried food and drinks
in packs stick to the tray. She eats tortillas, as
well. It is easy to stuff them with good things.

Ellen uses a sleeping bag like this one.
With straps like these, you can't fall out.

How can astronauts sleep if everything floats? They use sleeping bags that stick to the side of the spacecraft. They just float into the bag and strap themselves in. Then it is time to curl up and sleep tight!

Ellen Ochoa is dressed for space.

Ellen worked hard to be an astronaut. She went to college. She learned a lot of math and science. Then she went to school to learn about space flight. She had to pass a lot of tests. At last, she was an astronaut. Ellen thinks that she has a great job! Do you think so, too?

CA Critical Thinking

- What do you think Kitten in *Kitten's First Full Moon* might do in a space module?

- How are Kitten and Ellen Ochoa alike?

✓**Adjectives**

An **adjective** is a word that tells more about a person, place, or thing.

Write About the Sky

Julie wrote about the night sky.

The Night Sky

I think the night sky is so pretty. The dark sky is filled with tiny golden dots. These are the stars. Sometimes I try to count them.

Your Turn

Think about the sky in the day or at night.

What does it look like?

What does it make you think?

Write about the sky.

Writer's Checklist

☑ Did I write about what the sky looks like?

☑ Did I tell what the sky makes me feel or think about?

☑ Did I use adjectives to help me describe the sky?

What Scientists Do

Talk About It

What is a scientist?
What kinds of
questions do
scientists ask?

LOG ON ▶ Find out more about
what scientists do at
www.macmillanmh.com.

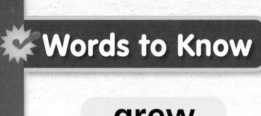

Words to Know

grew

knew

would

house

---

curious

idea

Read to Find Out

What makes the
seed look big?

Be Curious

Are you **curious**? Do you like to look at things that are little? Then this **idea** is for you.

Fill a bowl or glass with water. Then put something very little in your hand. Any little thing will work. This girl has a seed.

Next put your hand at the back of the bowl or glass. Does the little thing look like it **grew**? I bet you **knew** it **would**.

Do this with more things at your **house**. They will look big, too!

Genre

A **Biography** is the true story of a person's life.

Summarize

✓ **Make Inferences**

Use your Inference Chart.

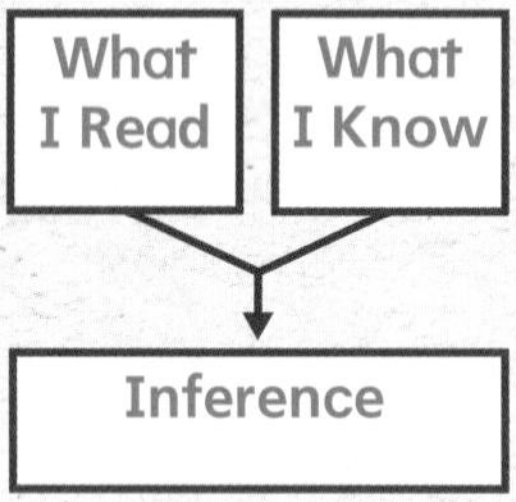

What I Read	What I Know

↓

Inference

Read to Find Out

What makes Ben Franklin a great American?

Meet Ben Franklin

by Philip Dray
illustrated by John Kanzler

Award Winning Author

Chapter 1

"Ben! Ben!" his friends called.

"Here I am," said Benjamin Franklin.

Ben was sitting on the docks. He was looking at the big ships. He liked the way the wind filled the sails.

Ben Franklin lived long ago. He liked to do many things. He liked to read. He was good at telling jokes and playing games.

Ben was a **curious** boy. He was smart, too.
He liked to dream. And he liked to make things.

One day, Ben made a red kite.

"This kite will be like the sails on the big ships,"
Ben said.

The next time Ben went for a swim, he had his kite with him.

"What will you do with that?" his friends asked.

"You will see," said Ben.

Ben ran with the kite. The wind lifted it.
He jumped into the water. He started to go
fast. The kite was pulling him!

"Look at Ben go!" said his friends.

"How did Ben think of that?" they asked.

63

Chapter 2

Time went by. Ben **grew** up. He still liked to dream. He still liked to make things.

He made a new kind of stove. This new stove was little, but it gave off lots of heat.

Ben made a new kind of glasses. They helped people to see up close and far away.

"How did Ben think of that?" people asked.

When Ben lived, people did not know much about electricity.

Ben was curious about it. He **knew** it could make sparks. He sometimes saw the sparks when he put his key into a lock.

One day it was raining. Ben looked at a flash of lightning. It looked like a big spark. He wanted to know if that flash was electricity.

Chapter 3

"How can I find out if lightning is electricity?" Ben asked. "I can not go up in the sky."

Ben had an **idea**. A kite had helped him long ago. A kite could help him again.

"I can not get up there," he said. "But a kite can."

The next time it looked like rain, Ben went out. The sky was dark. Ben had a kite and an iron key. He sent the kite up.

Lightning flashed. Ben felt the kite string shake. He saw sparks of electricity jump off the key.

"This shows that lightning is electricity!" said Ben.

Ben had an idea. He knew that if lightning struck a **house**, it could catch on fire. He put an iron rod on top of his house.

"Lightning will strike the iron rod, but not my house," Ben said. "The rod will keep my house safe."

Ben's friends put up iron rods, too.
Today we still put them on our houses
so they will be safe.

Ben was glad that the lightning rods helped people. In his life, Ben Franklin **would** do many more things to help people. He had more things to dream about and more things to make.

Meet Philip Dray

Philip Dray says, "I write books about Americans who do brave things to make our country better. I wanted to tell the story of Ben Franklin and his kite because he had the courage to try something no one had ever tried before."

 LOG ON ▶ Find out more about Philip Dray at **www.macmillanmh.com.**

 Author's Purpose

Philip Dray wanted to write a true story about Ben Franklin and his new ideas. Write about one of Ben's inventions. Tell how it made life better.

Critical Thinking

Retell the Selection

Use the Retelling Cards
to retell the selection in order.

Retelling Cards

Think and Compare

1. What kind of friend do
   you think Ben Franklin
   would be? Tell why.

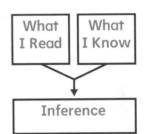

2. What things in your home
   use electricity?

3. Why do you think Ben Franklin is a
   famous and honored American?

4. What did you learn to do in
   "Be Curious"? How is it like what
   Ben Franklin did?

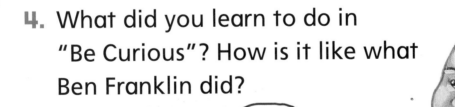

A Close Look

How do **scientists** see tiny things up close? They look through a **microscope**. That makes tiny things look big.

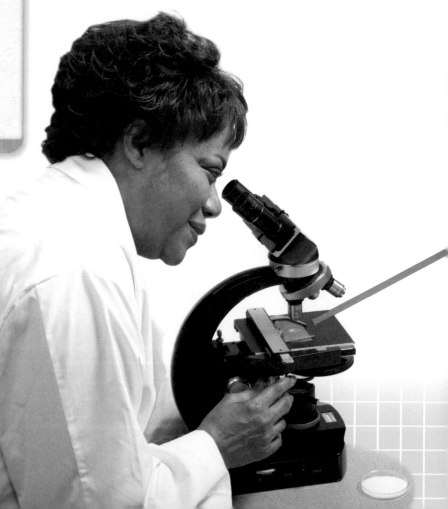

Look at the **photograph** in the circle.
It was taken with a microscope. It
shows things you see each day.
Can you tell what it is?

This is **salt**. Now you can see the
shape of each grain.

This is **hair**. You might have as many as 100,000 hairs on your head. Each hair has a hard coating.

This is a blade of **grass**. Sharp edges help keep bugs off.

What else would you like to see close up?
What do you think it would look like?

 Critical Thinking

What could young Ben Franklin have done with a microscope?

Write a Report

✓ **Adjectives that Compare**

Add -*er* to adjectives that compare two. Add -*est* to compare three or more.

Kevin wrote about one of Ben Franklin's inventions.

Ben invented a lightning rod. He saw lightning burn a house. He put an iron rod on his roof. Lightning struck it and not the house. It was one of his greatest inventions.

Your Turn

Find out about one of Ben Franklin's inventions.

Think about what the invention does.

Write a report about why it was important.

Writer's Checklist

☑ Did I tell what the invention was and why it was important?

☑ Do the adjectives that compare end with -er or -est?

☑ Did I use short sentences and long sentences?

Talk About It

What kinds of weather do you know about? What is your favorite kind of day?

LOG ON ▶ Find out more about the weather at www.macmillanmh.com.

What's the Weather?

warm

sound

their

know

great

---

extreme

predict

Warm and Cold Days

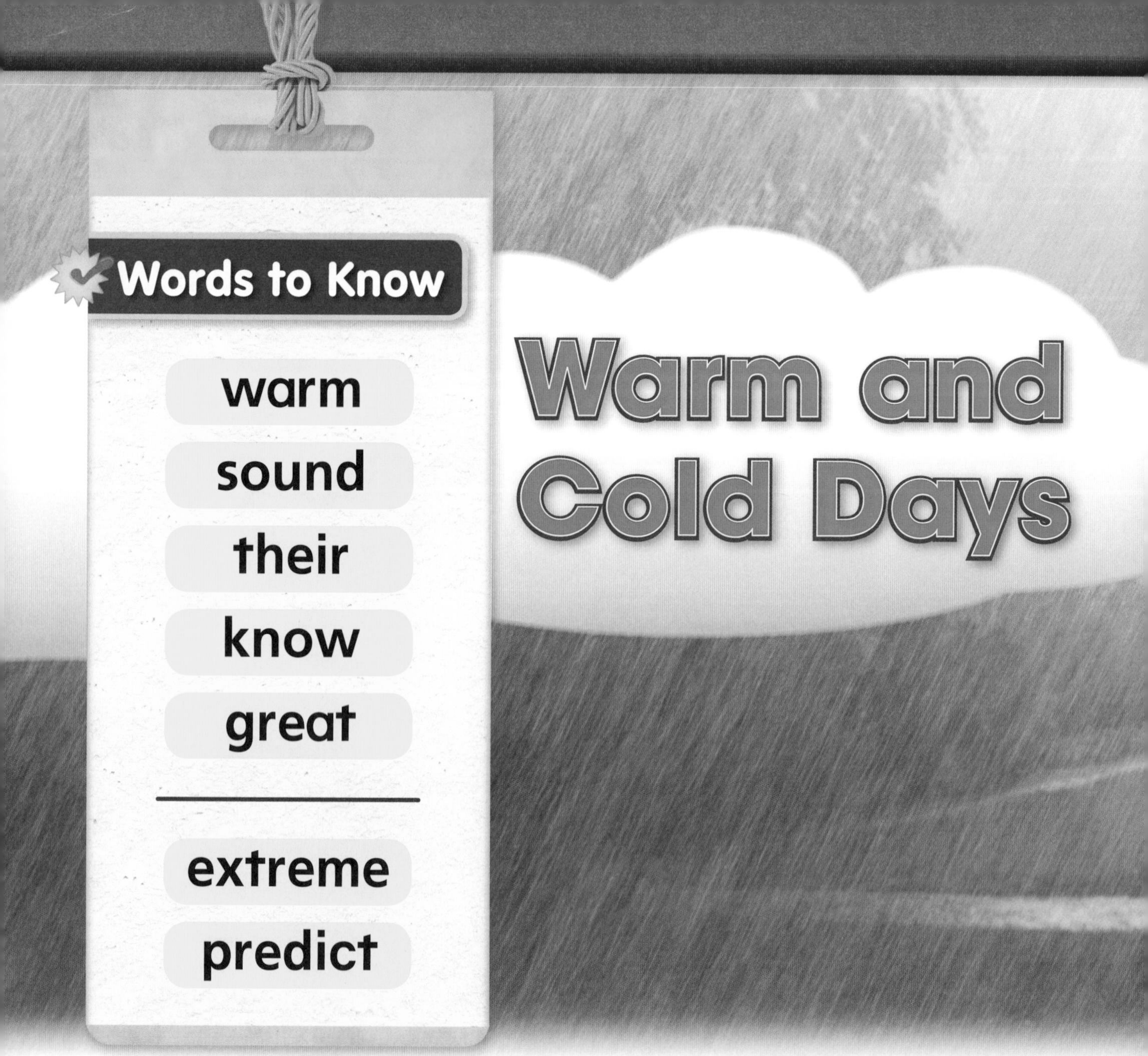

What is this day like? It is **warm** and wet. The rain makes a nice **sound**. Kids play in **their** homes.

This rain is **extreme**. But it will stop. Can you **predict** how the day will be then?

This day is cold. But these kids **know** how to stay warm. They run and jump and have a lot of fun. What a **great** day to play!

85

Stormy Weather

How many sorts of storms do you **know** about?

There are all sorts of storms. Which storms do you see where you live?

86

On some days, the sky is gray.
That might mean a storm is
on the way.

A gray sky can mean rainstorms. You may see **great** flashes of lightning. Next comes a loud **sound**. That is thunder. It's time to go inside!

Lightning can make a tree catch fire.

Thunderstorms may have strong winds. The winds can blow branches off trees. Balls of ice may fall from the sky. This is hail. It can hail when it is **warm** or cold.

Most hail is small. Some is bigger than a tennis ball. ▶

Some storms come when it is very cold. It can snow so much that you can't see. Strong winds can blow snow into big piles. This is a blizzard.

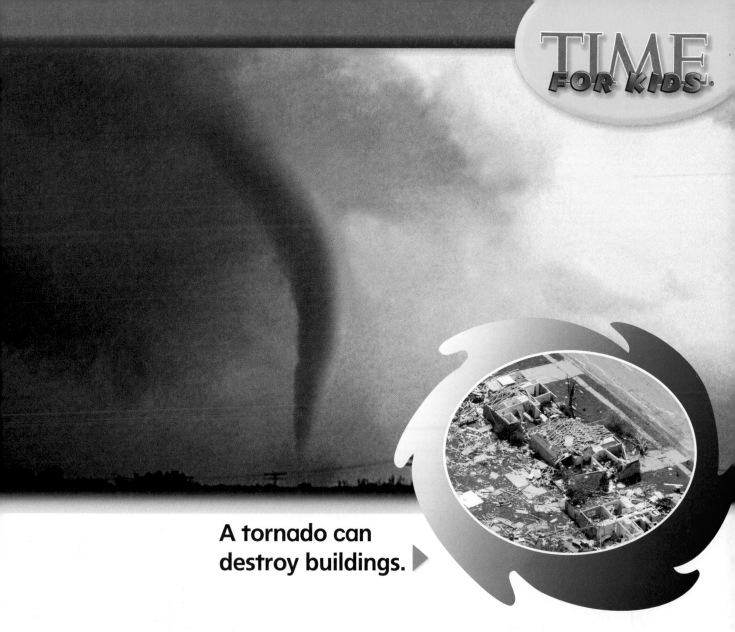

**A tornado can
destroy buildings.**

Some storms have **extreme** winds.
Tornadoes are made of fast winds that
spin and spin. The winds can pick up
trucks and homes.

Scientists have ways to **predict** when
tornadoes will come. Then people can
get out of **their** way.

What is the weather like today?
Does it look like a storm is on its
way? Or is it a great day for playing
outside?

Critical Thinking

Tell What You Learned

What did you learn about storms?

Think and Compare

1. How are a thunderstorm and a blizzard the same? How are they different?

2. Tell about a storm you have seen. How was it like the storms you just read about?

3. What would you do if you were caught in a blizzard, thunderstorm, or hailstorm?

4. How are the storms in "Stormy Weather" and "Warm and Cold Days" alike?

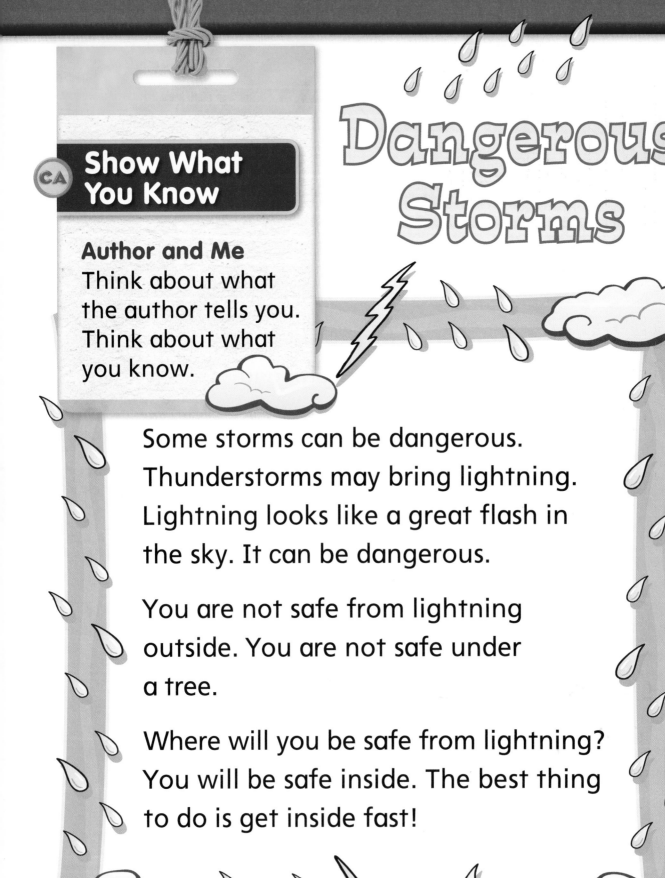

Author and Me
Think about what the author tells you. Think about what you know.

Dangerous Storms

Some storms can be dangerous. Thunderstorms may bring lightning. Lightning looks like a great flash in the sky. It can be dangerous.

You are not safe from lightning outside. You are not safe under a tree.

Where will you be safe from lightning? You will be safe inside. The best thing to do is get inside fast!

Go on ▶

Directions: Answer the questions.

1 Which picture shows lightning?

A   B   C

2 Why are thunderstorms dangerous?

A The rain will make you wet.

B The thunder is very loud.

C They bring lightning.

> **Tip**
> Think about what you know.

3 Where would you be safe from lightning?

A in your classroom

B on a river

C in the park

Write About the Weather

Rudy made a plan. Then he wrote a report about a tornado.

TORNADOES

A tornado is a very strong kind of storm. It looks like a spinning cloud. The top of a tornado is in the sky. The bottom touches the ground. Tornadoes are dangerous.

CA Your Writing Prompt

Everyone has seen a storm of some kind.

Think about a storm you've seen or heard about.

Write a report on what this storm was like.

Writing Hints

☑ Give your report a title.

☑ Describe what the storm looked like and sounded like. Tell what the storm did.

☑ Check your report for mistakes.

The Seasons

What seasons do you have where you live? What is your favorite season?

LOG ON ▶ Find out more about seasons at www.macmillanmh.com.

Words to Know

yellow

orange

against

below

fall

sure

---

wondered

season

Read to Find Out

Why is fall a fun season?

A Fun Season

"Let's play catch," said Liv.

"First we have to rake the leaves," said Dad.

Dad and Liv raked. There were red leaves, **yellow** leaves, and **orange** leaves.

Dad leaned his rake **against** a tree.

"Is it time for catch?" **wondered** Liv.

Then Dad started to run. He jumped up and landed in a big pile of leaves.

"Jump in, Liv!" Dad shouted.

Liv jumped as high as she could.

"Look out **below**!" she shouted.

"**Fall** is a fun **season**," said Dad.

"It **sure** is!" said Liv.

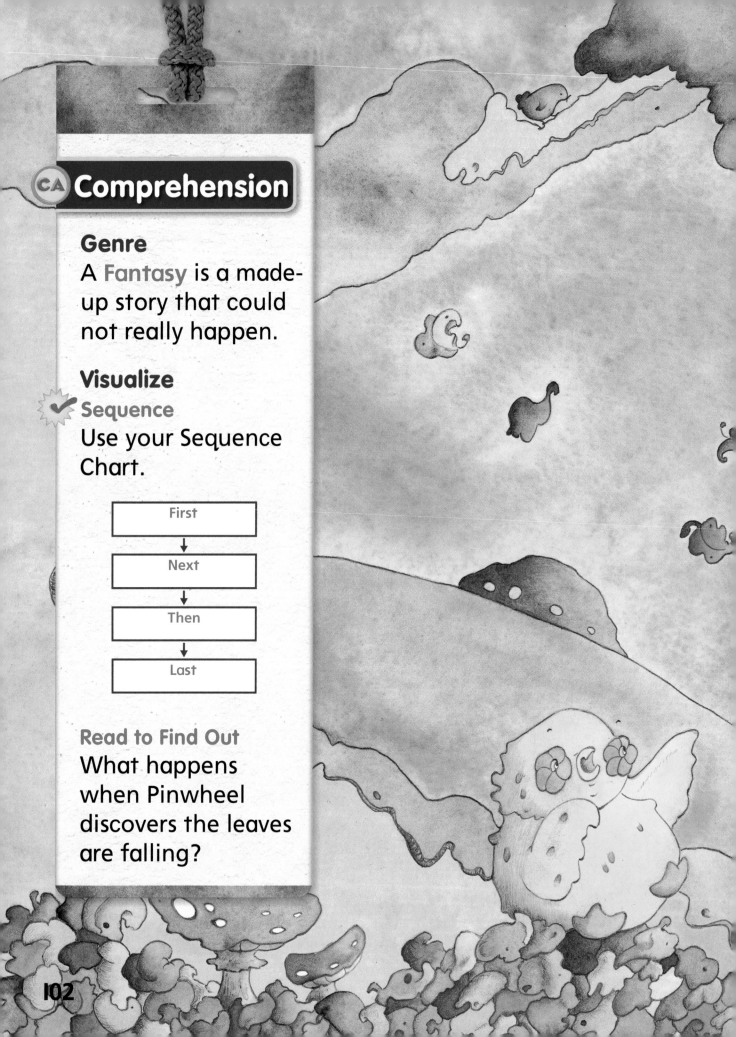

CA Comprehension

Genre
A Fantasy is a made-up story that could not really happen.

Visualize

Sequence
Use your Sequence Chart.

First
↓
Next
↓
Then
↓
Last

Read to Find Out
What happens when Pinwheel discovers the leaves are falling?

Happy Fall!

from Pinwheel Days

by Ellen Tarlow • illllustrated by Gretel Parker

Pinwheel was waiting for Squirrel.

"I like Squirrel and Squirrel likes me,"
he sang.

"Pinwheel! Be quiet!" came a voice.

"I am trying to sleep."

It was Owl.

"I am sorry, Owl," said Pinwheel.

Pinwheel felt an itch.

He rubbed **against** the tree.

"Pinwheel!" shouted Owl.

"Stop bumping the tree!
My bed is shaking."

"I am sorry, Owl," said Pinwheel.

Pinwheel stood as still as he could.

Something soft touched his head.

"What is that?" he **wondered**.

He shook his head.

A red leaf fell.

The wind blew.

More leaves fell.

"1, 2, 3, 4, 5," Pinwheel counted.

"Oh, no!" he said. "I broke the tree."

"Hello, Pinwheel," said Squirrel.
"Squirrel, I broke the tree!
Owl is going to be so mad at me!"
cried Pinwheel.

"Are you **sure** it's broken?"
asked Squirrel.
The wind blew.
More leaves fell.
"6, 7, 8, 9, 10," Pinwheel counted.
"See?" he said. "Broken."
"Very broken," said Squirrel.
They looked up.
More leaves fell.
"Go back!" they shouted.

But the leaves kept on falling.

Red leaves.

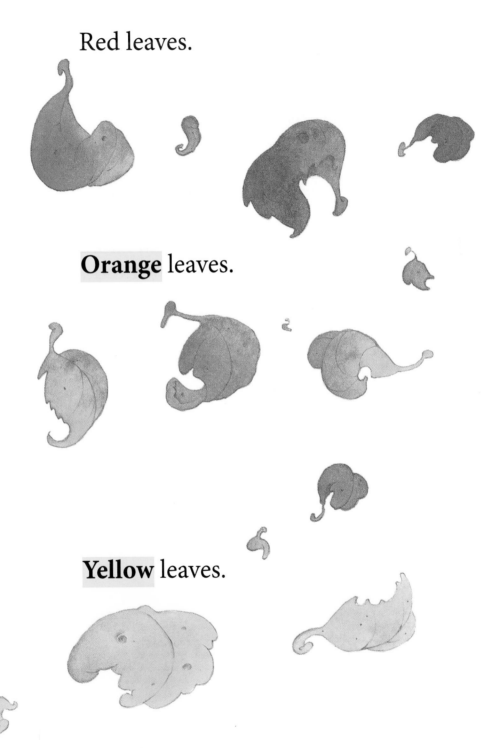

Orange leaves.

Yellow leaves.

There were too many to count.

"You won't like it down here,"
Pinwheel told the leaves.
"You will only get stepped on,"
said Squirrel.
"And squashed," added Pinwheel.
"Very squashed," said Squirrel.
"Let's show them," said Pinwheel.
"Good thinking," said Squirrel.
He climbed up the tree trunk.
"Look out **below**!" he shouted.
He jumped into a pile of leaves.
"See?" Pinwheel told the leaves.
"Squashed!"

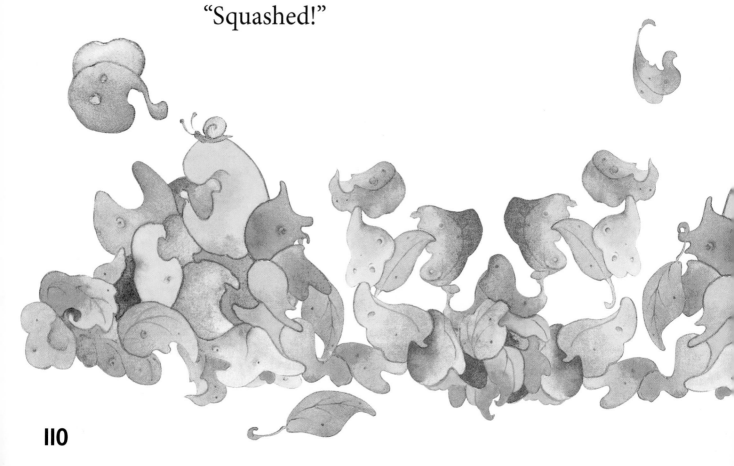

Then he heard laughing.
"Pinwheel," laughed Squirrel.
"Jump in!"

Squirrel popped out of the leaves.
He jumped back in.

Then Pinwheel jumped in.
"Catch me!" called Squirrel.

"Be quiet, you two!" shouted Owl.

He stepped out of his house.

He looked around.

"Ah, **fall**!" he said.

He looked down.

"Hide!" said Squirrel.

"Where?" asked Pinwheel.

"Look out below!" called Owl.

He jumped into the leaves.

"Run!" said Squirrel.

But it was too late.

"Hello," said Owl. "Happy fall!"

"Fall?" asked Pinwheel.

"Fall?" asked Squirrel.

"It's my favorite **season**," said Owl.
Pinwheel looked at the colorful
leaves.
"Happy fall!" he shouted as loudly
as he could.
Then he jumped in to find Squirrel.

Meet Pinwheel's Pals

Ellen Tarlow has always loved stories about talking animals. She got the idea for Pinwheel after seeing a photograph of a baby donkey.

Gretel Parker got her first real paint box when she was four. She has been painting animals ever since. Her favorite character in "Happy Fall!" is Owl because "he looks a bit cross at first but is very kindhearted, really."

Another book by Ellen Tarlow and Gretel Parker

Pinwheel Days
By Ellen Tarlow
Art by Gretel Parker

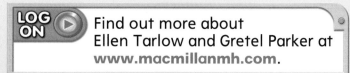

LOG ON ▶ Find out more about Ellen Tarlow and Gretel Parker at **www.macmillanmh.com.**

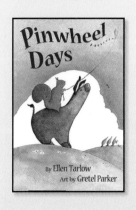

(CA) Author's Purpose

Ellen Tarlow got the idea for Pinwheel after seeing a donkey in a photograph. Make up a character based on an animal you have seen. Write about your character.

Critical Thinking

Retell the Story

Use the Retelling Cards
to retell the story in order.

Retelling Cards

Think and Compare

1. What happens when Pinwheel first feels a leaf fall? What happens next?

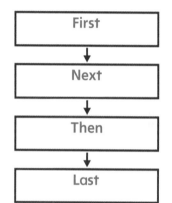

First
↓
Next
↓
Then
↓
Last

2. Have you ever had a silly idea like Pinwheel's? What was it?

3. What is fall like where you live?

4. How do Pinwheel and Squirrel act like Liv and Dad in "A Fun Season"?

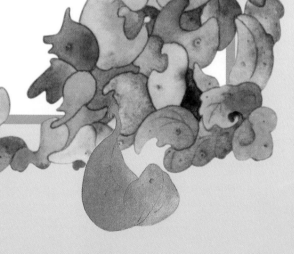

Science

Genre
Nonfiction gives information about a topic.

Text Feature
Some Diagrams show the order in which things happen.

Content Vocabulary
summer
winter
animals

LOG ON ▶ Find out more about seasons at **www.macmillanmh.com**.

SEASONS

A season is a time of year. There are four seasons in a year. They are spring, **summer**, fall, and **winter**.

In spring, the weather gets warmer. The days stay light longer. It may rain a lot in spring. The sun and rain help plants grow. Many **animals** are born in spring. There is a lot for them to eat then.

In spring, leaves on trees start to come out.

Summer comes after spring. Summer has the most daylight. That means more time to play outside! The weather gets hot in a lot of places. Plants grow big in summer. Animals eat and grow big, too.

In summer, the leaves on trees get bigger.

Fall follows summer. There is less daylight in fall. The weather starts to get colder. Plants stop growing. Some animals save food for when it will get much colder. Other animals go where they will find more food.

In fall, leaves may turn red, yellow, and orange.

In many places, winter is cold. It may snow. There is not much for animals to eat. So some animals, such as bears, sleep in winter. They will wake up in spring when they can find food.

In winter, trees have no leaves. They will grow again in spring.

Look at these trees. How do they change over a year? What do the trees tell us about each season?

CA Critical Thinking

- What is Owl's favorite season?

- What might Pinwheel and Squirrel play in winter, spring, and summer?

Write a Poem About a Season

✓ **Color Words**

Color Words are adjectives that tell the color of a place or thing.

Ruby wrote a poem about spring.

In spring, the rain comes
Down, down, down!
But then flowers come up.
Red, yellow, pink flowers.
All the colors come
Up, up, up!

Your Turn

Write a poem about a season you like.

Tell something special that happens in that season.

Use words to describe how the season looks, feels, sounds, or smells.

Writer's Checklist

☑ Did I tell something special about a season?

☑ Did I use words to describe the season?

☑ Did I use color words correctly?

How do baby animals change as they grow up?

 Find out more about growing animals at **www.macmillanmh.com**.

Watching Animals Grow

127

eyes

learn

open

enough

air

————————

cub

wild

Read to Find Out

How do bear cubs change as they get older?

A Cub Grows Up

When a bear **cub** is born, its **eyes** are closed. But it does not need to see to eat. The tiny cub drinks milk. It does not need to **learn** how because it just knows how. Soon its eyes **open**. After a while, the cub is strong **enough** to go out into the fresh **air**.

Then it is time to go out into the **wild**. The cub learns to hunt and to catch fish. The cub also learns what is best to eat from plants. Soon the cub will be grown up. Then it will take care of itself.

Comprehension

Genre
Nonfiction gives information about a topic.

Summarize
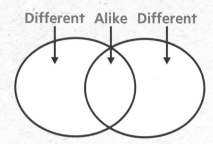

Compare and Contrast
Use your Compare and Contrast Chart.

Different   Alike   Different

Read to Find Out
How is a tiger cub different from a grown-up tiger?

A Tiger Cub Grows Up

by Joan Hewett

photographs by
Richard Hewett

In the Nursery

Tara is a tiger **cub**.

She was born in a **wild** animal park.

The cub is hungry.

She feels the tip of the bottle.

She drinks her warm milk.

When Tara is
9 days old,
her **eyes open**.

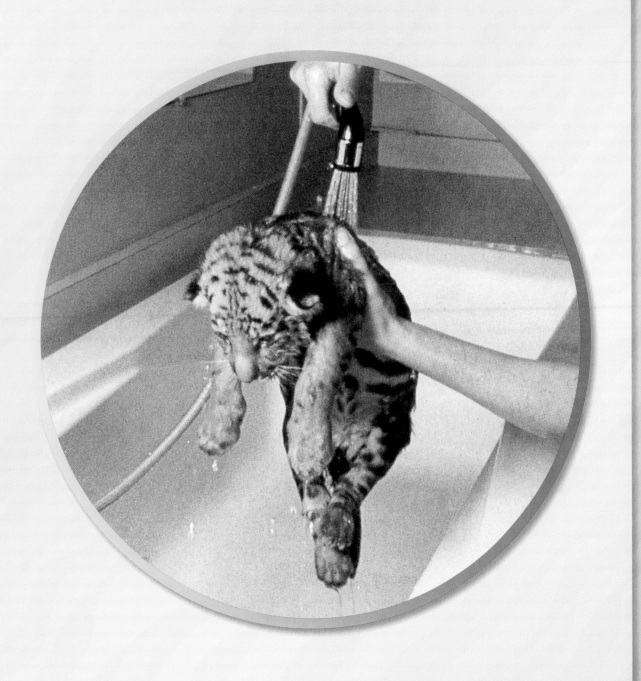

Grown-up tigers like to swim. But little Tara
does not like her first bath.

Mary feeds Tara.
She talks to the tiger cub.
She gives her kisses.

At night, Mary takes the cub home with her.
Tara drinks her milk.
She falls asleep.

Then Tara wakes up.
She is hungry!
She wants more milk.

Tara drinks until her belly is full.
She falls back to sleep.
As she sleeps, she grunts
and squeals.

Tara is 3 weeks old.
Her baby teeth are coming in.
She has pointed teeth for tearing meat.

And she has rounded teeth for chewing.

Chewing feels good. But a plastic tray
is hard to hold with chubby paws.

Each day, Mary shows the cub a piece of meat.
Tara does not want to try it. Not yet!

Playtime is a time to **learn**.
Can Tara crawl over Mary's legs?
How hard will Mary let her bite?

Tara is 3 months old. Mary takes Tara to the
animal doctor. It is time for a checkup.

The bright lights are scary. The tiger cub roars.

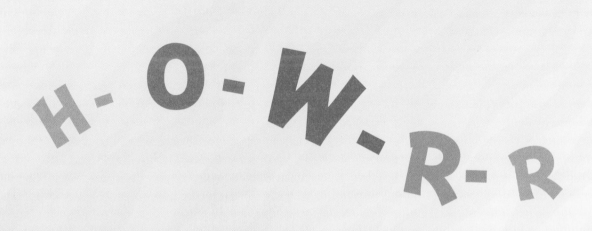

Tara Goes Outdoors

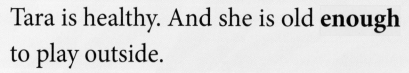

Tara is healthy. And she is old **enough** to play outside.

Grass and sky seem strange to Tara.
The **air** is filled with new smells.
The tiger cub follows her nose.
She runs across the grass.

Lynn takes care of Tara now.
Lynn hugs Tara. She plays with Tara.
She shows her falling leaves.

Lynn plays with Tara every day.
She teaches Tara what she can do.
She teaches Tara what she cannot do.

Tara greets Lynn with a friendly chuffing sound. Lynn returns the greeting.

Climbing over Lynn is fun.
Following Lynn is fun.
Tara creeps along the ground.
Then she pounces!

Tara Joins the Grown-up Tigers

Tara is 9 months old. She is big and strong.
She can join the park's grown-up tigers.
Tara likes her new home. She can run across
the grass. She can climb on logs. She can
nap under leafy trees.

Tara watches the big tigers swim.
She walks around the pond. It is hot.
So Tara jumps in. Tara is 1 year old.
The tiger cub has grown up.

S·P·L·A·S·H

Watching Animals with the Hewetts

Joan Hewett thinks research is the most difficult, interesting, and fun part of writing. Many of her books are about baby animals living in zoos or rescue centers.

Richard Hewett says, "I think children's books are the best." He often takes photographs for books written by his wife, Joan Hewett.

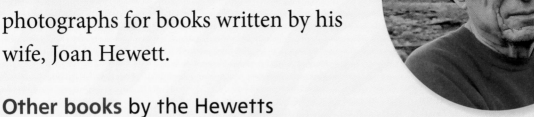

Other books by the Hewetts

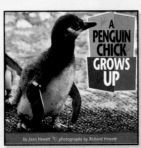

A HARBOR SEAL PUP GROWS UP

by Joan Hewett   photographs by Richard Hewett

A PENGUIN CHICK GROWS UP

by Joan Hewett   photographs by Richard Hewett

LOG ON ▶ Find out more about Joan Hewett and Richard Hewett at **www.macmillanmh.com.**

CA Author's Purpose

Joan Hewett wanted to give information about a baby animal. Write about a baby animal you know. Tell how it changed as it grew.

Critical Thinking

Retell the Selection

Use the Retelling Cards
to retell the selection in order.

Retelling Cards

Think and Compare

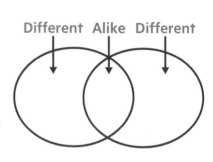

Different Alike Different

1. What is Tara like when she
   is a baby? How is she
   different at nine months old?
   How is she the same?

2. What was the most
   interesting thing you
   learned about tigers?

3. Can a one-year-old child
   take care of itself like a
   one-year-old tiger? Why
   or why not?

4. How are Tara and the cub
   in "A Cub Grows Up" alike?

(CA) **Poetry**

Genre
A Poem uses words
that sound good
together.

Literary Element
Word Play
Poets often use
words in fun and
interesting ways.
This is called word
play.

 Find out more about
growing animals at
www.macmillanmh.com.

The Tiger

by
Douglas Florian

I am a cat – come hear me purrrr.
I've many stripes upon my furrrr.
I speed through forests like a blurrrr.
I hunt at night – I am tigerrrr.

CA Critical Thinking

How is the tiger in this poem different from the tiger in *A Tiger Cub Grows Up*?

Write About Vets

Chris wrote about why vets are important.

Take your pet to the vet. Vets help sick pets. But even if your pet is not sick, you should go. The vet checks your pet and does lots of tests. Your pet should go to the vet one or two times a year.

Your Turn

How does a vet take care of animals?

Why is it important to take a pet to the vet?

Write about what a vet does and why vets are important.

Writer's Checklist

☑ Did I tell what a vet does?

☑ Did I tell why it's important to take a pet to the vet?

☑ Did I use number words correctly?

✓ **Review**

Compare and Contrast
Sequence
Compound Words
Chart
Bold Print

What Grasshopper Learned

Grasshopper played music all day long. "Will you play with me, Ant?" he asked.

"I don't have time for such things," said Ant. "I must find food for winter, and make my home."

"But it isn't cold yet," said Grasshopper. So he kept on playing, while Ant worked hard.

160

One day, there was a snowstorm. The snow swirled and the wind howled.

Ant had plenty of food and a cozy home. Grasshopper had nothing to eat. He was cold!

Ant gave Grasshopper a bit of corn. "I hope you learned your lesson," said Ant.

Grasshopper sighed. "Thank you, Ant!" he said. "I learned that I must plan ahead."

What Does the Weather Chart Say?

The weather is what it is like outside. It may be **hot**, **warm**, or **cold**. Can you see **sun**, **rain**, or **clouds**? Can you feel the **wind**?

A class made a weather chart. The pictures show what the weather was like on each day.

sun   rain   clouds

snow   wind

Use the pictures to read the weather chart.

1 What was the weather like on Monday?

2 When did it rain?

3 On which days do you think the class played outside?

4 Which day was good for flying kites?

Monday	Tuesday	Wednesday	Thursday	Friday
4	5	6	7	8

CA Critical Thinking

Now answer the questions. Base your answers on the story "What Grasshopper Learned."

1 **What does Grasshopper do FIRST?**
   A cook
   B play music
   C make a home

2 **Which word is a compound word?**
   A winter
   B snowstorm
   C cozy

3 **What happens after it gets cold out?**
   A Grasshopper gets hungry.
   B Grasshopper goes on a trip.
   C Grasshopper keeps playing music.

4 **What do you think Grasshopper learned?**
   How did he learn it? Write about it.

Now answer the questions. Base your answers on the story "What Does the Weather Chart Say?"

1 How are Tuesday and Thursday the SAME?
- A They are both stormy.
- B They are both sunny.
- C It is raining on both days.

2 How can you tell it is windy on the chart?
- A The sun is shining.
- B There are clouds.
- C The trees are swaying.

3 What kinds of words are in bold print?
- A words that name the days
- B words that name the weather
- C words that name animals

Write on Demand

PROMPT How are a snowy day and a rainy day the SAME? How are they DIFFERENT? Write as much as you can and as well as you can.

Glossary

What Is a Glossary?

A glossary can help you find the meanings of words. The words are listed in alphabetical order. You can look up a word and read it in a sentence. Sometimes there is a picture.

cub

planet

Sample Entry

Letter

Main Entry

Sentence

O o

open

A crocodile can **open** its mouth wide.

. photographs

Aa

against

The raindrops splashed **against** the window.

air

In the garden, the **air** smelled like flowers.

animals

Elephants are one of the biggest **animals**.

another

If there's no wind, we'll fly kites **another** day.

astronaut

An **astronaut** may travel to the moon.

Bb

below

From the airplane, the houses **below** looked tiny.

Cc

climbed

The squirrel **climbed** the tree.

cub

A lion **cub** stays near its mother.

curious

I am **curious** about polar bears.

Ee

enough

There was **enough** pizza for everyone.

extreme

A snowstorm is one kind of **extreme** weather.

eyes

This cat has yellow **eyes**.

Ff

fall

We like to watch the rain **fall**.

full

The pot is **full** of stew.

Gg

great

We had a **great** time at the park.

grew

Many plants **grew** in the garden.

Hh

house

I live in a red **house**.

Ii

idea

It's a good **idea** to wear your seat belt.

Kk

knew

I **knew** how to write my name when I was five.

know

Do you **know** how to whistle?

Ll

leaped

The rabbit **leaped** onto the rock.

learn

I want to **learn** about dinosaurs.

lucky

I feel **lucky** to have good friends.

Mm

microscope

Matt can see things up close with this **microscope**.

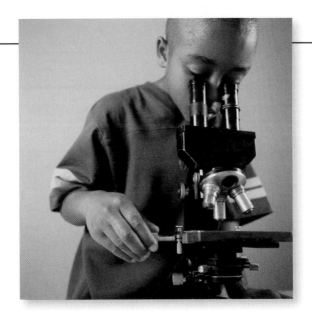

Oo

open

This crocodile can **open** his mouth wide.

orange

The pumpkin is a bright **orange** color.

Pp

photographs

Chris likes to take **photographs** with his new camera.

planet

Saturn is a **planet** with rings.

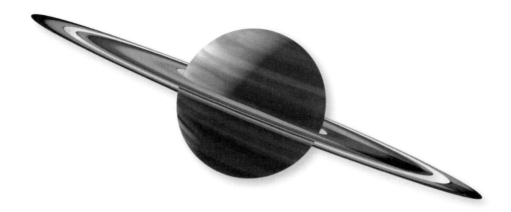

poor

The **poor** chipmunk ran from the swooping owl.

predict

The weather report may **predict** snow.

Ss

scientists

The **scientists** are working hard to discover new things.

season

Spring is the **season** when flowers start to bud.

sound

Thunder makes a loud **sound**.

summer

In **summer,** the lake is warm enough to swim in.

sure

Are you **sure** you fed the puppy?

Tt

their

My neighbors have **their** own swing set.

through

The sun peeked **through** the clouds.

Ww

warm

My new jacket is **warm**.

weightless

It would be fun to be **weightless** for a day.

wild
A **wild** animal finds its own food.

winter
It snowed this **winter**.

wondered
Pete **wondered** if he spelled the word correctly.

would
I **would** like to eat lunch before we play.

Yy

yellow
The ducklings are all **yellow**.

Acknowledgments

The publisher gratefully acknowledges permission fo reprint the following copyrighted material:

"Happy Fall" from *Pinwheel Days* by Ellen Tarlow, illustrations by Gretel Parker. Text copyright © 2007 by Ellen Tarlow. Illustrations copyright © 2007 by Gretel Parker. Used by permission of Star Bright Books, Inc.

Kitten's First Full Moon by Kevin Henkes. Copyright © 2004 by Kevin Henkes. Used by permission of Greenwillow Books, an imprint of HarperCollins.

A Tiger Cub Grows Up by Joan Hewett, photographed by Richard Hewett. Text copyright © 2002 by Joan Hewett. Photographs copyright © 2002 by Richard Hewett. Reprinted by permission of Carolrhoda Books, Inc., a division of Lerner Publishing Group.

"The Tiger" by Douglas Florian from *Mammalabilia: Poems and Paintings* by Douglas Florian. Copyright © 2000 by Douglas Florian. Reprinted with permission of Harcourt Children's Books.

Book Cover, A HARBOR SEAL PUP GROWS UP by Joan Hewett, photographs by Richard Hewett. Text copyright © 2001 by Joan Hewett. Photographs copyright © 2001 by Richard Hewett. Reprinted by permission of Carolrhoda Books, Inc., a division of Lerner Publishing Group.

Book Cover, A PENGUIN CHICK GROWS UP by Joan Hewett, photographs by Richard Hewett. Text copyright © 2004 by Joan Hewett. Photographs copyright © 2004 by Richard Hewett. Reprinted by permission of Carolrhoda Books, Inc., a division of Lerner Publishing Group.

ILLUSTRATIONS
Cover Illustration: Anton Petrov

8–9: Constanza Basaluzzo. 10–43: Kevin Henkes. 44–49: John Kaufmann. 56–75: John Kanzler. 100–101: Lizzy Rockwell. 102–117: Gretel Parker. 124: Ken Bowser. 129: Tom Leonard. 156–157: Tom Leonard. 160–161: Melissa Sweet.

PHOTOGRAPHY
All Photographs are by Ken Cavanagh or Ken Karp for Macmillan/McGraw Hill (MMH) except as noted below.

Inside Front Cover: Goodshoot/Alamy; 2–3: Ann Cutting/Jupiter Images. 3: Charles Volkland/AGE Fotostock. 4: Scott W. Smith/Animals Animals. 5: Bettmann/CORBIS. 6–7: John Kelly/Getty Images. 44–46: Courtesy of NASA.

47: Dorling Kindersley. 48: Courtesy of NASA. 49: Courtesy of NASA Kennedy Space Center (NASA-KSC). 50: image 100/PunchStock. 51: Bill Brooks/Masterfile. 52–53: Jose Luis Pelaez, Inc./CORBIS. 74: Courtesy of Philip Dray. 77: (cr) Davies & Starr/Getty Images; (c) Andrew Syred/Science Photo Library/Photo Researchers. 78: (tl) Steve Gschmeissner/Photo Researchers; (br) Stephen Marks/Getty Images. 79: (tl) Dennis Kunkel/Phototake; (tr) David Sacks/Getty Images. 80: Banastock/Imagestate. 81: Philadelphia Museum of Art/CORBIS. 82–83: Panoramic Images/Getty Images. 84: Derek Davies/Getty Images. 85: (bkgd) C Squared Studios/Getty Images; (t) AP Wide World. 86: Jim Cummins/Getty Images. 87: Peter N. Fox/AGE Fotostock. 88: John Henshall/Alamy. 89: (c, inset) Jim Reed/Photo Researchers; (b) Stockbyte/PunchStock. 90: AP Wide World. 91: (t) Warren Faidley/CORBIS; (cr) ©REUTERS/Jeff Mitchell/Newscom. 92: (tr) Richard Hutchings/Photo Edit; (cl) David Hanover/Getty Images. 92–93: DAJ/Getty Images. 95: (tl) Joel Sartore/Getty Images; (tc) Grafton Marshall Smith/CORBIS; (tr) Warren Faidley/CORBIS. 96: Comstock/Jupiter Images. 98–99: Bonnie Nance/Dembinsky Photo Associates. 116: Courtesy of Gretel Parker. 119: (b) Jan Halaska/Photo Researchers; (bkgd) Ariel Skelley/Getty Images. 120: (b) Jan Halaska/Photo Researchers; (bkgd) Comstock/PunchStock. 121: (t) Comstock/PunchStock; (b) Jan Halaska/Photo Researchers. 122: (b) Jan Halaska/Photo Researchers; (bkgd) Blend Images/PunchStock. 123: (all photos) Jan Halaska/Photo Researchers. 124: Dick Luria/Getty Images. 125: D. Hurst/Alamy. 126–127: Tom Murphy/National Geographic Image Collection. 128: Carl R. Sams II/Peter Arnold. 131–153: Richard Hewitt. 154: (tl) Courtesy Joan Hewett; (cr) Courtesy of Richard Hewitt. 158: Michael Newman/Photo Edit. 159: Arthur Tilley/Getty Images. 162: (cl) Digital Archive Japan/Alamy; (c) Rainman/zefa/CORBIS; (cr) Royalty-Free/CORBIS; (bl) Frank Krahmer/Masterfile; (br) Jim Reed/CORBIS. 163: (l to r) Digital Archive Japan/Alamy; Rainman/zefa/CORBIS; Royalty-Free/CORBIS; Frank Krahmer/Masterfile; Jim Reed/CORBIS. 166: (cr) Jeremy Woodhouse/Masterfile; (bl) Denis Scott/CORBIS. 167: (t) Royalty-Free/CORBIS; (b) Mastefile Royalty Free. 168: Jack Hollingsworth/Getty Images. 169: Jeremy Woodhouse/Masterfile. 170: (t) Yann Arthus-Bertrand/CORBIS; (b) Timothy Shonnard/Getty Images. 171: Joseph Sohm; ChromoSohm Inc./CORBIS. 172: Layne Kennedy/CORBIS. 173: (t) Ryan McVay/Getty Images; (b) Royalty-Free/CORBIS. 174: (t) Mastefile Royalty Free; (b) Denis Scott/CORBIS. 175: David Joel/Getty Images. 176: Rommel/Masterfile. 177: Image Source/Getty Images.

Reading/Language Arts
CA California Standards
Grade 1

READING

1.0 Word Analysis, Fluency, and Systematic Vocabulary Development
Students understand the basic features of reading. They select letter patterns and know how to translate them into spoken language by using phonics, syllabication, and word parts. They apply this knowledge to achieve fluent oral and silent reading.

Concepts About Print

1.1	Match oral words to printed words.
1.2	Identify the title and author of a reading selection.
1.3	Identify letters, words, and sentences.

Phonemic Awareness

1.4	Distinguish initial, medial, and final sounds in single-syllable words.
1.5	Distinguish long-and short-vowel sounds in orally stated single-syllable words (e.g., *bit/bite*).
1.6	Create and state a series of rhyming words, including consonant blends.
1.7	Add, delete, or change target sounds to change words (e.g., change *cow* to *how*; *pan* to *an*).
1.8	Blend two to four phonemes into recognizable words (e.g., */c/ a/ t/* = cat; */f/ l/ a/ t/* = flat).
1.9	Segment single-syllable words into their components (e.g., */c/ a/ t/* = cat; */s/ p/ l/ a/ t/* = splat; */r/ i/ ch/* = rich).

Decoding and Word Recognition

1.10	Generate the sounds from all the letters and letter patterns, including consonant blends and long-and short-vowel patterns (i.e., phonograms), and blend those sounds into recognizable words.
1.11	Read common, irregular sight words (e.g., *the, have, said, come, give, of*).
1.12	Use knowledge of vowel digraphs and *r-* controlled letter-sound associations to read words.
1.13	Read compound words and contractions.
1.14	Read inflectional forms (e.g., *-s, -ed, -ing*) and root words (e.g., *look, looked, looking*).
1.15	Read common word families (e.g., *-ite, -ate*).
1.16	Read aloud with fluency in a manner that sounds like natural speech.

Vocabulary and Concept Development

1.17   Classify grade-appropriate categories of words (e.g., concrete collections of animals, foods, toys).

2.0   Reading Comprehension

Students read and understand grade-level-appropriate material. They draw upon a variety of comprehension strategies as needed (e.g., generating and responding to essential questions, making predictions, comparing information from several sources). The selections in *Recommended Literature, Kindergarten Through Grade Twelve* illustrate the quality and complexity of the materials to be read by students. In addition to their regular school reading, by grade four, students read one-half million words annually, including a good representation of grade-level-appropriate narrative and expository text (e.g., classic and contemporary literature, magazines, newspapers, online information). In grade one, students begin to make progress toward this goal.

Structural Features of Informational Materials

2.1   Identify text that uses sequence or other logical order.

Comprehension and Analysis of Grade-Level-Appropriate Text

2.2   Respond to *who, what, when, where,* and *how* questions.

2.3   Follow one-step written instructions.

2.4   Use context to resolve ambiguities about word and sentence meanings.

2.5   Confirm predictions about what will happen next in a text by identifying key words (i.e., signpost words).

2.6   Relate prior knowledge to textual information.

2.7   Retell the central ideas of simple expository or narrative passages.

3.0   Literary Response and Analysis

Students read and respond to a wide variety of significant works of children's literature. They distinguish between the structural features of the text and the literary terms or elements (e.g., theme, plot, setting, characters). The selections in *Recommended Literature, Kindergarten Through Grade Twelve* illustrate the quality and complexity of the materials to be read by students.

Narrative Analysis of Grade-Level-Appropriate Text

3.1   Identify and describe the elements of plot, setting, and character(s) in a story, as well as the story's beginning, middle, and ending.

3.2   Describe the roles of authors and illustrators and their contributions to print materials.

3.3   Recollect, talk, and write about books read during the school year.

WRITING

1.0 Writing Strategies Students write clear and coherent sentences and paragraphs that develop a central idea. Their writing shows they consider the audience and purpose. Students progress through the stages of the writing process (e.g., prewriting, drafting, revising, editing successive versions).

Organization and Focus

1.1	Select a focus when writing.
1.2	Use descriptive words when writing.

Penmanship

1.3	Print legibly and space letters, words, and sentences appropriately.

2.0 Writing Applications (Genres and Their Characteristics) Students write compositions that describe and explain familiar objects, events, and experiences. Student writing demonstrates a command of standard American English and the drafting, research, and organizational strategies outlined in Writing Standard 1.0.
Using the writing strategies of grade one outlined in Writing Standard 1.0, students:

2.1	Write brief narratives (e.g., fictional, autobiographical) describing an experience.
2.2	Write brief expository descriptions of a real object, person, place, or event, using sensory details.

WRITTEN AND ORAL ENGLISH LANGUAGE CONVENTIONS

The standards for written and oral English language conventions have been placed between those for writing and for listening and speaking because these conventions are essential to both sets of skills.

1.0 Written and Oral English Language Conventions Students write and speak with a command of standard English conventions appropriate to this grade level.

Sentence Structure

1.1	Write and speak in complete, coherent sentences.

Grammar

1.2	Identify and correctly use singular and plural nouns.
1.3	Identify and correctly use contractions (e.g., *isn't, aren't, can't, won't*) and singular possessive pronouns (e.g., *my/ mine, his/ her, hers, your/s*) in writing and speaking.

Punctuation

1.4	Distinguish between declarative, exclamatory, and interrogative sentences.
1.5	Use a period, exclamation point, or question mark at the end of sentences.
1.6	Use knowledge of the basic rules of punctuation and capitalization when writing.

Capitalization

1.7	Capitalize the first word of a sentence, names of people, and the pronoun *I*.

Spelling

1.8	Spell three-and four-letter short-vowel words and grade-level-appropriate sight words correctly.

LISTENING AND SPEAKING

1.0 Listening and Speaking Strategies Students listen critically and respond appropriately to oral communication. They speak in a manner that guides the listener to understand important ideas by using proper phrasing, pitch, and modulation.

Comprehension

1.1	Listen attentively.
1.2	Ask questions for clarification and understanding.
1.3	Give, restate, and follow simple two-step directions.

Organization and Delivery of Oral Communication

1.4	Stay on the topic when speaking.
1.5	Use descriptive words when speaking about people, places, things, and events.

2.0 Speaking Applications (Genres and Their Characteristics) Students deliver brief recitations and oral presentations about familiar experiences or interests that are organized around a coherent thesis statement. Student speaking demonstrates a command of standard American English and the organizational and delivery strategies outlined in Listening and Speaking Standard 1.0.
Using the speaking strategies of grade one outlined in Listening and Speaking Standard 1.0, students:

2.1	Recite poems, rhymes, songs, and stories.
2.2	Retell stories using basic story grammar and relating the sequence of story events by answering *who, what, when, where, why,* and *how* questions.
2.3	Relate an important life event or personal experience in a simple sequence.
2.4	Provide descriptions with careful attention to sensory detail.